Called

By Victoria Therman

DEDICATION

"HERE I RAISE MY EBENEZER,
HITHER BY THY HELP I'VE COME.

LET THY GOODNESS, LIKE A FETTER
BIND ME CLOSER LORD TO THEE.

PRONE TO WANDER, LORD, I FEEL IT
PRONE TO LEAVE THE GOD I LOVE.
HERE'S MY HEART LORD,
TAKE AND SEAL IT
SEAL IT FOR THY COURTS ABOVE."
......Robert Robinson, 1758 (1735-1790)

Hannah gave birth to a son. She named him Samuel, saying,

"Because I asked the Lord for him."

When Samuel was weaned from Hannah, his mother, she fulfilled her vow to dedicate him to God. *(Story in found in 1 Samuel, Chapter 1)*

Lord, this is Your handiwork, and I, Your humble messenger. This book is wholly dedicated to You to be used for Your glory and honor.

Not I, but Christ...

ACKNOWLEDGEMENT

This book has been a journey in the making. I have started and stopped so many times over the years, I have lost count. I've now come to believe that with each step, I was still running as I poured out bits and piece of the struggle to be "good" on my own and in my own strength, yet never quite winning the race.

His grace is truly sufficient. His strength is indeed perfect.

Because of His grace, I am able to maintain a very positive relationship with my ex-husband and his family. His family is still my family and they have embraced my new husband Robert (Rob) as family.

Speaking of husband, THANK YOU! My husband, Rob, learning of my story - this message that I have hidden away inside for so long, pushed and prodded...encouraging me to take up my love for writing and storytelling. "Hun, just do it! Go for it! It's what you love. Do what you love." Thank you my darling.

Elder Courtney Williams... my pastor, brother, and friend, now deceased, "saw into me" and heard my "loud cry" long before I knew what this was. God sent a man who pursued his appointed mission: Help her to see! How I miss you, my brother and friend. I miss our long conversations as we searched the scriptures to see if it is so (Acts 17:11).

My children, who, through parenting, demonstrated to me the most beautiful story ever written – God's love for us...HIS children. My amazing children have taught me so much about myself...and my understanding of God's Love. And now, I can say with assurance, I know who holds their tomorrows...and I know who holds their hands!

CONTENTS

"I have called you by name, you are Mine."

Isaiah 43:1

THE CALL

I pushed forward with the crowd charging up the hill, careful to steal quick glances backwards at the hell and destruction behind me. The atmosphere was hot, steaming, it was almost impossible to breathe. The heat simmered and swirled in front of us. The ashes from the burning landscape created a winter-like effect interlaced the ash flakes from the charred remains falling all around us. The remnants of the world and life as we know it were disappearing right in front of us. The flames took no prisoners. Everything and *everyone* in its' path were being consumed.

"Keep moving forward!" "Move!" "Faster!" "Move!"

The shout sounded like someone from far back. The crowd pushed and jostled against each other, desperate to get as far up the hill as possible. I could feel someone's hand on my back shoving me forward, forcing me to move faster than my legs could keep up. There was terror, frozen in streaks on faces, eyes averted, scared to look at each other but knowing through an unspoken consensus that we must get to the top of the hill, and quickly.

"Move faster! Move faster, it's coming up fast!"

The urgency in her tone caused the crowd to push harder against each other with a stronger force demanding that the climb pick up speed quickly!

I was moving as fast as I could among the throng, grabbing at those around me when I felt like I was falling, scrambling to keep up the pace - it was difficult. It took everything in me to move with the flood of bodies around me, but I had to, for fear of being trampled. It was all about survival, and everyone wanted to survive, regardless of the cost.

"Do not follow the crowd; go to the Rock."

I glanced up quickly to see if others were following the new directives.

No one even bothered or even appeared to have heard the command.

I swiftly looked around, careful not to miss my steps or pace behind the person in front of me, hoping to make eye contact with the voice who spoke the new escape plan...every head was lowered and sheltered by arms from the merciless heat with clear intentions to stay on track.

So, like a lemming, I ignored the command and kept moving forward with the herd of people, pushing forward, and fighting to get as far up the hill and away from the burning inferno that traveled with relentless sureness behind us.

The flames devoured the landscapes, homes, trees, rocks, bodies of water as if they were never there. The screams could be heard from those who didn't move quickly enough. Those who tried to save their belongings packed too much, and now struggled under the weight as they tried to escape what appeared to be the extensively wide gaping mouth of hell. Those who were not able to move fast enough out of its path announced the result. The ear-splitting scream would tell when someone succumbed to the angry, ruthless flames.

"Don't follow the crowd; go to the Rock!"

The voice was louder and more insistent now. Again, I braved the heat in my face and looked around for acknowledgement from the others. Again, not one person looked, or acknowledged the voice. The inferno was gaining ground as it snarled its way over the hills destroying every object and life form in its path.

I know I heard screams closer to me this time, screams that told of another person who didn't move fast enough. The fear climbed upward in my body was almost immobilizing, but somewhere, somehow, I knew that stopping was not the answer.

"Karlean! STOP! Don't follow the crowd. Move to the left. Go to the Rock; you will be safe there. Go now! If you follow this path, you will die."

Stopping so suddenly almost proved to be a horrible idea. I was nearly run over by the teeming crowd fighting reach the crest of the hill. We all believed that over that hill we would all be safe. Over that hill, we will be rescued. Over that hill, the fire could not come.

No other thought process went beyond getting over the hill. We just knew we had to get to the top - and over.

I took a tentative step forward in line with the crowd. I knew I heard the voice, and what was most striking, is that the voice knew me personally - I was called by my name given to me by my parents at birth.

Another tentative step forward then I turned my head and looked to the left. I could see the rock, but it looked so far away. I thought about the time I would lose trying to change course now to get to the rock, and if I would even make it, pushing through the crowd moving in a different direction. I could be trampled!

My steps were no longer tentative as I picked up my pace with the crowd. It would be sure death to try to make it across that wide expanse overflowing with possibly millions of people running for safety. I decided to stay and take my chance with the crowd.

"Karlean! You will surely die if you stay on this course. Karlean, run to the Rock and live."

Without another thought - without verifying who heard the command and who didn't, without second-guessing how I would make it to the rock before I was consumed by the raging fire, or trampled by the frightened sea of people, I turned and moved towards the rock.

I was fearful to question the authenticity of the voice and the command. Something inside me trusted it. I turned, pushing and shoving my way across the expanse of land, screaming as loud as I could.

"Come with me to the rock and you will be safe!

My eyes scanned the crowd of people as I pushed against the terrified crowd. I hoped someone would validate my sanity and move with me. Everyone was focused on getting over that hill regardless of what stood in the way and right now, I was definitely in the way.

Follow me! The rock is safe; we won't die there, but we will die here."

Someone pushed me out of the way. Others sidestepped me without the slightest acknowledgement. I even heard snide remarks.

"Why don't you just go! Idiot!"

I was shoved hard to move out of the way. I would have to do this alone – I was going to the rock by myself.

———————— ◦⊂⊃◦ ————————

With renewed energy and purpose, I made the heavy, tiring, trek towards the rock, which was no easy feat! The heavy smoke had us all coughing and wheezing; Everyone's eyes were swollen, red and watering. Some were gasping for air. Some were asking others for a drink of water. People appeared to be trapped in a mindless stupor, just stumbling along, not cognizant of what was truly happening or where they were going. Survival was the name of the game, and everyone wanted to survive.

It was frightening. Deadly frightening. I am not sure how I knew, but I did - the whole world was on fire, the earth was being consumed by fire. I wasn't quite sure how it began, but somewhere in the pit of my stomach, I knew there was no safe place. Not even over that hill.

The closer I got to the rock, the more defeated I felt. The sheer height, width and overall size of the rock had me baffled. For me to be safe I would need to get on top of it, so the fire could not reach me, but HOW? It was as if Mount Everest was rolled up in a huge ball and sat in the middle of the earth. I couldn't climb this. There was no place to grip. THIS was the safety the voice spoke of. *Run to the rock and live.* What will stop this fire from consuming me standing beside the rock?

Is the fire not already consuming every other rock, boulder, and mountain in its path?

Why did I listen? Why am I over here all by myself?

Defeat softened my bones and my knees felt rubbery. I leaned against the rock and slid to the ground. I was tired, frustrated, and terrified. I was thirsty too but couldn't tell if I was hungry. I must have been, but for some reason, the thought of food nauseated me.

I needed to get up and figure out another way - I knew I should because the screams were much louder now and if I stretched my neck upwards, I could see the orange glow of the flames as they licked their hungry, unrelenting way forward. It was only a matter of time.

I should get up and try to move, but, somehow, I knew I needed to stay here and wait. Maybe rest for a while.

Tucking my body as close to the rock as possible, I curled into the curvature of it, my back to the madness all around me. I immediately nodded off to sleep - I was tired. Let me rest, then I'll figure out what I need to do next - but first... let me rest.

"Then the Lord awoke me from sleep, like a warrior overcome by wine."

Psalm 78:65

AWAKENED

I woke up in a soaking dread. My nightgown clung to my drenched body. Looking around, I recognized my room with the light-yellow walls and white curtains. My stuffed toys were displayed on the white day bed with the pretty floral cover in the corner.

I looked towards the window, feeling fear dry up my mouth. What was left outside? How many died? How did I get back to my house? My room? My bed? How did I still have a house? *Did the fire miss my house?*

I tiptoed across the room to the window, expecting to see charred ruins all around; instead, everything was as I last remembered. The manicured lawns with the trimmed flowers, just the way my mother liked it, were all intact… how was that possible? How could I explain what I endured, what seemed like, a moment ago; what I saw, heard, and felt with what I am seeing now? *What actually happened?* I felt utterly confused.

At the age of 10, I knew I had dreamed something awful but could not bring myself to share it with anyone. I didn't know *how* to explain it to anyone without sounding crazy. If I said the world was on fire, the next question would surely be, *"how would you know the world was on fire?"*

That was a question I could not answer…. I just knew in my dream it was the whole world.

I moved about my daily life with apprehension, unsure what to expect. I became sensitive to a candle flame - the danger, the damage, the fluidity. Its dread, its destruction. The screams … the smell.

In the Caribbean, sugarcane farmers would set fire to harvested fields, before they planted the next crop. Smells intermingled; charred earth, burned stubs of sugarcane, dried leaves and stalks, and burned sugar. I liked the smell; I found it comforting.

After my dream, it was no longer so. Every flame sent shivers up and down my body, creating a tenseness that lasted for hours, sometimes days, until I felt some semblance of safety again.

I grew quiet and fretful. The slightest unexplained sound rattled me and finally, after weeks of living in my own private hell, I told my mother of the dream. I was surprised I could still recount the specifics with clarity and accuracy.

"It was a nightmare; that's what happens when you eat late at night."

Caribbean parents' explanation for every nightmare is always due to late night snacks, even if you *didn't* have a late-night snack! If mom says that's what it is, then that is exactly what it is...and be done with it.

Easier said than done.

Days, weeks, months, years, passed and without meaning to remember or think about the dream, I would be reminded and again with clarity and accuracy as if I had dreamed it at that very moment.

See? I just told you about the dream with the same clarity and accuracy!

I don't recall my 21st birthday being an eventful day - there was no party to celebrate my entrance into this new phase called womanhood.

Uneventful. Dressed in black, wearing raggedy sweats and bulky shoes! That was my birthday.

I went to bed early, praying for the day to end. I wanted to wake up and my birthday had passed, bringing on the new day, forgetting the day before. I could handle that until the next birthday.

I smelled the fire as it raged forward, devouring everything in its path. How could something so beautiful be so destructive? Bright reds, oranges, low yellows and soft blues, all glowed beautifully. Growing up with a father whose trade as a tailor allowed me to see fabric with all these colors to varying degrees, I learned to love and appreciate the splendor of colors - just not hot and deadly.

Screams and shouts for everyone to move faster and climb higher could be heard over a stampede of running feet as the whole world tried to climb to the other side of the hill. Louder still was the same voice telling me to run to the rock and be saved; the same voice begged me to stop moving with the crowd but to run to the rock. Same dream. Same details. Same rock where I curled my body for a quick rest before I continued.

I did not wake up with a start this time. I knew outside was unchanged; same as when I went to bed. There was no need to race to the window to check what was left outside. I knew it was not a nightmare because I ate late - I didn't eat at all the night before.

So, what was it? Why did this dream repeat itself in the exact details eleven years later?

I wondered if this had ever happened to anyone else. Was this even normal? Or maybe a warning that my home was going to burn to the ground, or that a fire will bring an end to me? It felt like a warning, but a warning of what?

I knew deep down that this dream meant much more than I was acknowledging.

I was afraid.

I wasn't sure what I was afraid of, but I was scared.

I was terrified.

"Oh, how great is Your goodness, which You have laid up for those who fear You, which You have prepared for those who trust in You in the presence of the sons of men!"

Psalm 31:19

THE GOODNESS

So often I hear people talk about knowing the very moment God called them. They can pinpoint the place, the occasion, even the hour when they heard HIS voice, or felt HIS distinct presence and when they made the decision to live for God.

I had heard people talk about situations they had been in that brought them to the knowledge that God was in their story, or had placed a special calling on their lives.

At the young age of 10, how could I have known that HE was calling me, or *had* called me?

Being raised in a Baptist home with a praying mother does not qualify as a family living for God.

Church was a requirement for my mother's children, but I believed we went to church each week more out of duty than a desire to build a relationship with the Lord.

I was also pulled by the music. Church music was a different kind of music.

Each week I went to church eagerly anticipating the arrangements of the choir and any special guest singers. Occasionally dad would go with us, mostly on Easter, Christmas, and New Year's Eve, just those special days. Possibly to remind God that he still remembered Him, and where the church was. Though it was not a requirement for him, he still made sure we went with mom every Sunday.

I'm not sure I understood what was happening around me or why; all I knew is that each week after church, mom would sing and hum for days. Going to church made her feel good, it made me feel good too.

Going to church also had a positive effect on us for a few days after church service, we were the most obedient children on planet earth! We didn't talk back or defy our parents, especially mom. We were perfect kids…. until midweek when the goodness wore off and we were back to being rowdy kids with me as the rebel.

Whatever mom said not to do, that is *exactly* what I would do. Nothing extreme, nothing crazy, just pushback. Then the next church service and the music would renew me, and I would be perfectly obedient.

Though at some points it didn't seem like it, especially when I left home, I never forgot the goodness

To this day I never forgot the goodness.

"God is our refuge and strength, an ever-present help in trouble."

Psalm 46:1

AN EVER-PRESENT HELP

Marriage, kids, college, in that order. My relationship with God found its place in my life, growing with each experience and at times diminishing with others. The elevator ride effect of my Christian life with its highs and lows, ebb, and flow, did not go unnoticed by me. How true it is that you can lie to others but never to yourself. Whether truth or lie, a relationship with God was so vital to me that I carved out a space and time weekly, sometimes daily for our private conversations. On a weekly basis I would go to church, even if it was just to hear the choir, a special singer…. or a message in song.

The early years of my marriage were difficult. Two young people in love, but clueless as to what it means to "set up house." Every day was driven by the naked, shameless need to survive. There was no such thing as reserve funds – every last dime was accounted for, even then it was still not enough.

I did everything I could to make ends meet. In addition to my regular jobs as an office assistant for a doctor's office, and a Substance Abuse Counselor for a Methadone Program at the local hospital, I also cleaned houses, baby-sat children, and went to school full time working towards increasing my education. My husband worked hard too, but I learned very early that my husband's passion would not push him to pursue any other avenues for income other than photography. I respected his passion and dedication, so I settled myself in the role as the "go-getter," the "hustler." *(That's the Caribbean in me!).*

I know this may sound strange, but I was neither bitter nor angry. I simply understood who we were and what we needed to do to survive and stay happy. Did you catch that word, *"stay?"* Because we were! We were happy with each other.

Our "penthouse" apartment was our haven. That's what the landlady called it when she rented us that sparsely furnished, 1-bedroom attic for $750.00 per month. I know that doesn't sound like a lot of money in today's time, but back in the early 1990's, that was a lot of money for a 400-square-foot space. Especially since some of the space was unusable, those areas closest to the walls where the roof sloped. I recall my husband not being able to sit on the toilet in an upright position and would have to lean forward for fear of bumping his head. Me? Not so much! At 5ft. 2inches, small spaces sometimes work in my favor!

The landlady was a Christian and attended the same church as we did, which was the clincher for us in renting the apartment. Being around like-minded people of faith was so very important to me, especially someone older that fitted the "motherly" role. I also loved the neighborhood, with its lovely, homes within walking distances to the shops, public transportation, even to church (when the weather was good).

We were settling in, adjusting to "our" normal. As I said, life was hard, but we managed and were happy.

Then my husband lost his one job. I doubled down at work, leaving home at 5:45 in the mornings and returning well after midnight. This became a regular routine – yet it was still not enough to cover all our bills and meet our needs. We ate scraps put together in such a way by my husband's skillful hands that it appeared we ate well every day! He was king of illusions when it came to the kitchen, and I loved him for that!

It was tax time and I could tell you; no one looked more eagerly to tax time than the working poor. (Jesus! Blessed be His name! I think this is the first time I have ever openly acknowledged that we were poor!).

The taxes were done, now for the waiting game... that mailman was our dearest friend as we looked for that amber-colored envelope in the metal, latticed mailbox each and every day.

It was a couple of months that we were not able to pay the full rent, and on the third month, that knock came at the attic door, the knock we knew would come but prayed it didn't until our tax returns came. The landlady told us with certainty, and a bit of annoyance, that she needed the full rent for the month along with all the back rent owing or we will have to leave the next month.

How would this be possible? If we could barely make a full month on just my salary, how were we to do this? We pretty much owed two full months' rent. I think that was my first bout with anxiety – it felt like a heart attack.

Over the next couple of weeks, we survived on almost nothing, saving every cent to pay all that we owed. We rarely drove, we bought food only when we HAD to and scraped together enough money, short of $362.00. We were out of time. We knew the landlady was not joking because she had stopped communicating with us face to face. The occasional note on the attic door (which would trigger my anxiety attacks) reminded us of the due date for *all* of the money.

I don't remember ever crying. I do recall getting quieter and quieter with each day and the evident weight loss of my husband and myself.

"Don't be afraid, for I am with You."

Isaiah 41:10

A SHELTER IN A TIME OF STORM

We walked to church that Sabbath morning. It wasn't because it was great weather, or that we needed exercise. We had a car and no gas, so we walked to church.

It was Father's Day service, and I remember the pastor preached a sermon about the husband being the High-Priest of his home; he is the protector, the prayer warrior that keeps his family at the cross of Jesus Christ, and the *provider* for his home.

My heart ached for my husband as I sat beside him, squeezing his hand, reassuring him that I was with him and that as long as we were together, we would be fine.

I tried with all of me to communicate my love, my devotion, my acceptance, my understanding, and my commitment to the marriage and to him through my hand that held tightly to his, his squeezing back with a sight tremble. A storm was brewing.

We were both afraid.

It was a very difficult sermon to listen to, especially for an unemployed husband.

After church, we decided against staying for lunch in the fellowship hall, though we would have greatly appreciated the food. We needed to go home and figure out our next move before Monday, the day all the current and back-owed money was due to the landlady.

It was a slow walk home and it was hot, which made the journey seem longer – I didn't mind. I was just not ready to face the landlady. So we slowed our pace, and admired other people's beautiful properties… other people's money… We relished our silent dreams.

We turned the corner and walked to the house. I wasn't looking for it, and neither was my husband. But as soon as we entered the gate, our eyes went immediately to the mailbox attached to the front porch of the house. There, sitting in the black latticed-style box, was a rectangular-shaped, amber-colored envelope. It was from the United States Department of Treasury. The only piece of mail in the box.

I started crying before I opened the envelope. I looked at my husband and saw his body sag from the relief. When I opened the envelope, the check was for the exact amount of the back rent to the penny. I cried harder because the check in my hand was evidence that God heard our prayers, HE saw our distress, HE felt our pain and our fear. He understood our hopelessness.

And He answered as only He can!

"Enter His gates with thanksgiving, and into His courts with Praise. Be thankful unto Him and Bless His name. For the Lord is good!"

Psalm 100:4

A GOOD PERSON: ISN'T THAT ENOUGH?

Growing up in a house of musicians, music became the second language spoken with frequency and fluency throughout my household. Dad played the bass, my brothers played the drums and guitar, and my mom, little sister, and myself sang.

Music was a keystone in our home, and we gathered there often, not really for worship. Eventually, the "worldly" music took on a sort of reverence for the instrumental arrangements, not so much the worldly lyrics, born out of our love for music. I didn't fully realize what was happening. Before long, the music bridged the invisible chasm, between the world and religion. This generated a deepening of faith, at least, for some of us.

My first opportunity to sing publicly came as no surprise; what was surprising was the ease with which I performed in front of a very large crowd. The amphitheater in the town square was filled, overflowing; I belted out *"She's Out of My Life"* by Michael Jackson... and with ease

I switched the noun from "she" to "he." I closed my eyes and felt the song. I didn't hear the music ...I *felt* it travel from the soul of my feet, up my legs and spine. Now I understand why some entertainers sing bare footed. You *really* feel the music!

———————— <——> ————————

I enjoy a good sermon as much as the next person – I enjoy sermons that caused me to take a closer look at myself the most, especially when it comes from a pastor that didn't scream, rant and rave theatrically, hoping to entertain instead of educate. However, it was never the sermons that pulled me to the church, it was always the music.

Gospel music tells a story, strips you of your secrets, leaves you naked and vulnerable, reaches deep within in such a way that breaks away all pretense and excuses...my silent scream normally started deep within and creeped up into my throat only to escape as a wretched moan as my tears flowed unchecked. It has always been the music – even now.

I think I heard the lapping of the flames before I felt the heat. I heard the flames as they moved across the expanse, forcing the crowd uphill screaming for those in front to move faster. With exactness and accuracy, the dream woke me up. Turning to look at my sleeping husband I scrambled out of bed, checked on the kids in their rooms to see if they were safe. I moved about the house quietly, staring at pictures hung on the walls, on tables, thinking about how time flies.

At thirty-seven years old, I had lived what I believe was a full life. A wife, a mother, a professional, I was not perfect. I won't tell you of my sins, my narrow escapes, my failures, my dark moments; because I know you know those moments well yourselves.

I understood the woman I was. I was fiercely devoted to my family, a hard worker, a mother who saw the world through the eyes of her amazing children, and a woman whose heart yearned for the Lord in such a way that I hungered for His connection. Feeling His presence mobilized me to do just about anything. Unfortunately, this connection was not a consistent one.

It is fair to say I knew what the problem was, but yet I blamed God. I questioned His love for me – I often screamed, *"If You love me, why won't You save me…even from myself?!"*

I wanted to be rescued without doing anything. I waited for a switch to be turned on then I would be the "perfect Christian," free from the pull of the world on my heart, my mind focused on God. I prayed and waited while I continued to live my life as best as I could, based on what I believed to be good.

For the most part, my life denied my faith; therefore it was weak but somehow, deep within me, my heart yearned for the God of my mother. Oh! She loved the Lord without apology or excuse. I loved the Lord too, but I used His love to excuse my faithlessness, then apologized later for the lack thereof.

I straddled the fence between the world and my Christian faith. I wanted so desperately to be a good Christian and yet, I also wanted the pieces of the world that made my life glow like a shiny new penny; a desire to feel elevated, important, with all its pomp and circumstance, while never letting go of the God I grew up knowing. Though sometimes a speck in my life, my faith never left me completely... and this created and fostered... nurtured even, a sense of guilt that ate at me with voracity

I hid from everyone in plain sight. Sounds hard, right? It's fairly easy because I learned quickly that no one really cares about, "How you're doing," or, "How is your day." It's just a pleasantry used to past time without seeming awkward or impolite.

The turmoil within me was my own private battle – the war raged as I fought for the goodness without having to sacrifice too much of who I was... I didn't quite understand (or maybe I didn't want to understand) that I was nothing without Him! Acknowledging this would mean change, and I didn't think I was a bad person so why did I need to change?

"A good person doesn't mean a "godly" person."

I can't recall where I heard that phrase, but I remembered it ricocheted in my head like a loud gong! I may have seemed good – but was I godly? Was I living for the Lord? That question caused me sleepless nights. That was the question I privately rebelled against. I won't go into the details of my personal rebellion and the things I did, but He knew my heart

SCREAMED for Him. For Him to come after me. To rescue me.

I was the BIGGEST hypocrite!

"Where can I go from your Spirit" Or where can I go from Your Presence? If I ascend into heaven, You are there; If I make my bed in hell, behold, You are there. If I take the wings of the morning, and dwell in the uttermost parts of the sea, even there, Your hand shall lead me."

Psalm 139:7-10

YOU CAN RUN BUT YOU CANNOT HIDE

"LIGHT AND DARKNESS CAN NEVER MIX." I can still hear my mother's high-pitched voice with the girlish lilt. "THE LIGHT WILL OVERCOME THE DARKNESS IF YOU LET IT." I was never afraid of the dark, I just preferred when I could control it.

I hate power outages, or "blackouts" as we called it in the Caribbean. My children have never quite understood my, *"dis-ease"* with power outages, especially when they would often see me sit in the dark quite comfortably. But that's a dark I could control with the flip of a light switch! With power outages, you are not in control of the darkness because the light switch will not bring light and end the darkness. Then, to me, the darkness is consuming and controlling.

What is interesting, and so very assuring, is that if you strike a match in that darkness, that small light consumes the vast darkness!

As much as my life shone with worldly glitter, a great job, a nice house and car, there was also a darkness that pushed to acknowledge itself. No matter how loudly I laughed, or how widely I grinned, even forced my eyes to crinkle; no matter how much I pretended to be the happiest person in the world, that darkness reminded me on a daily basis that I was lying to MYSELF.

"You Can Run but You Can't Hide."

That was the title of the sermon the pastor preached that Sabbath morning as I sat stony-faced in church with my two young children. My friend, Charm, and her daughter attended church with me. I pretended that the message meant nothing to me. I am not sure why I was trying so hard to disconnect; I normally listen for the message that is meant for just me.

Maybe it was the title of the sermon, or the way the pastor kept staring at me that got under my skin.

The sermon ended and it was now time to exit the sanctuary, time to "paint" my smile on my face and leave as quickly as I possibly could.

God had another plan.

I reached the pastor standing at the door, thanking everyone for attending and wishing everyone a happy Sabbath. I extended my hand to shake his but instead, he placed what appeared to be a scroll in my outstretched hand, smiling, while staring directly into my eyes and wishing me a happy Sabbath and hoping to see me soon. I quickly looked away and exited the building, almost racing to the parking lot for my car.

I moved quickly. I felt like I had come undone.

"What was that he gave you?"

My friend Charm, seated in the passenger seat asked as she eyed me, sensing my discomfort and noticing that I held tightly to the scroll.

"I have no idea." I responded without looking at her, my voice flat and matter-of-fact.

But I did. I had stared at it before rolling it back into a scroll. It was the very sermon the pastor had preached from.

I was very uncomfortable.

"You OK?" Charm asked, still eyeing me increasing my discomfort (if that was even possible).

"Of course! Why wouldn't I be?" I answered as flippantly as I could, struggling to not sound as out of breath as I felt.

"I just wanna go home and sleep for a while. It's been a long week. Thank God for the Sabbath!"

Conversation closed.

I popped in the CD and listened as Cee Cee Winans belted out **"Alabaster Box",** a song I have loved and identified with. (This is a whole different book all on its own).

Charm understood my intent to change the subject when I started singing along with the music. I think she knew the scroll in my hand was much more than I was letting on.

The pastor saw me. He saw *into* me. The Holy Spirit was speaking through him to me and I wasn't even aware. All I felt was the discomfort and "dis-ease" throughout his sermon and his repeated stares at me.

I want to believe he waited for me at the door as I came forward and shook his hand. I even want to believe God's hand reached out to me that day and tried to grab a hold of me.

But I ran; again, and again. I came to realize, over the years that with every nudge and every discomfort, I laced up my shoes and ran.

"Immediately there fell from his eyes something like scales, and he received his sight at once; and he arose and was baptized."

Acts 9:18

AND THERE WAS LIGHT!

"Tell me the stories of Jesus! I love to hear.

Things I would ask Him to tell me if He was here!

Scenes by the wayside,

Tales of the sea,

Stories of Jesus, tell them to me!"

William Henry Parker penned these lyrics in 1885, at the request of the children of his Sunday School Class, "Teacher, tell us another story!"

Can you imagine the fire in those tender hearts as they listened to their teacher tell beautiful, loving stories of Jesus? Can you see those upturned faces smiling, with eyes shining as they implored their beloved teacher to share more about Jesus' love for them?

The heart yearns to hear more and more stories of Jesus, as the scales from our eyes fall away and He *calls you out of darkness into His marvelous light!* (1 Peter 2:9)

Have you ever been hungry, starving even, but not really aware of it until you are given food to eat? That's how I felt when I came to the realization of what my dream meant, when the pastor explained that God had been calling and pursuing me all my life. I felt starved. And I hungered for Him... I wanted to feast on the pure manna from heaven!

Scales falling away from your eyes is said to mean that you have suddenly come to the realization of truth about something you did not quite understand, or you were somewhat deceived.

I didn't understand.

I had been deceiving myself.

I returned to church the very next Sabbath, and I continued until I left New York and relocated to North Carolina many years later. I had never heard the Word of God spoken in such a manner, coming *directly* from the Bible! It wasn't just my eyes that were opening – it was my heart.

It was months later when I "gingerly" shared my recurring dream with the pastor, who listed in rapt attention as I shared details as if it was happening as I spoke. With his head bowed, the occasional nod affirming he was listening, the pastor smiled and looked at me with renewed interest.

"Praise God!" He kept saying those, words over and over. With what appeared like tremendous effort he quieted himself, smiled deeply, and stared at me for a considerable amount of time.

"He has been calling you. He has been pursuing you. Don't run from Him. He wants to save you and He has a mighty work for you. Oh, my sister! He has a lifesaving work for you!"

OK! What a heavy responsibility! However, though scary it was the first time in my life that, regardless of all the people that loved me, and cared for me. That I felt really, really SPECIAL.

"Coming to the realization."

Do you have any idea how profound that statement is? Or what is it actually saying? As my mother used to say, *"You cannot un-know what you know."* There was no turning back from "knowing", because now that I know I am accountable for what I do. *"Therefore, to him who knows to do good and does not do it, to him it is sin."* (James 4:17).

I wish I could end here, and I say, *"and I rode off in the sunset into a perfect life!"* Not even close! I have blown it over and over...too many times to count. However I have His blessed assurance that I can, *"come boldly to the throne of grace, that I may obtain mercy and find grace to help in time of need."* (Hebrews 4:16).

No more running. Though challenging, intimidating and overwhelming at times, I now seek to press closer to My Father so I can experience the fullness of Him.

God has demonstrated His love and mercy throughout my life, and I have witnessed first-hand His might and power! The, "still small voice" so many of God's children speak of, I now listen for –rejoicing when I do hear it above the noise and clatter of everyday life. He does speak to us. He does! He truly loves to speak with us, and desires to do so. When you do hear Him…. *"Harden not your heart as in rebellion"* (Hebrews 3:15).

Heaven is a REAL place, and the invitation is extended to all who believe. *"For God so loved the world that He gave His only begotten Son, that* **whosoever** *believes in Him should not perish but have everlasting life!"* (John 3:16). You and I are both on His mind; He has never forgotten or forsaken us. How could He, when He left to prepare a place for us? He said so! *"In My Father's house are many mansions; if it were not so, I would have told you. I go to prepare a place for you. And if I go and prepare a place for you, I will come again and receive you to Myself; that where I am, there you may be also."* (John 14:2-3)

His Word is His bond and cannot come back to Him void. *"For as the rain comes down, and the snow from heaven, And do not return there, But water the earth, And make it bring forth and bud, That it may give seed to the Sower and bread to the eater, so shall My Word be that goes forth from My mouth; It shall not return to Me void, But it shall accomplish what I please, And it shall prosper in the thing for which I sent it."* (Isaiah 55:10-11)

What an assurance! What joy divine!

"Behold, now is the accepted time; behold, now is the day of salvation." (2 Corinthians 6:2)

...Speak Lord, Your servant is listening. (1 Samuel 3:10)

My Silent Prayer

1. Take my life and let it be
   Consecrated, Lord, to Thee.
   Take my moments and my days,
   Let them flow in endless praise.

2. Take my hands and let them move
   At the impulse of Thy love.
   Take my feet and let them be
   Swift and beautiful for Thee.

3. Take my voice and let me sing,
   Always, only for my King.
   Take my lips and let them be
   Filled with messages from Thee.

4. Take my silver and my gold,
   Not a mite would I withhold.
   Take my intellect and use
   Every pow'r as Thou shalt choose.

5. Take my will and make it Thine,
   It shall be no longer mine.
   Take my heart, it is Thine own,
   It shall be Thy royal throne.

6. Take my love, my Lord, I pour
   At Thy feet its treasure store.
   Take myself and I will be
   Ever, only, all for Thee.

Frances Ridley Havergal, 1874 (1836-1879)

Made in the USA
Middletown, DE
03 November 2023